D1287505

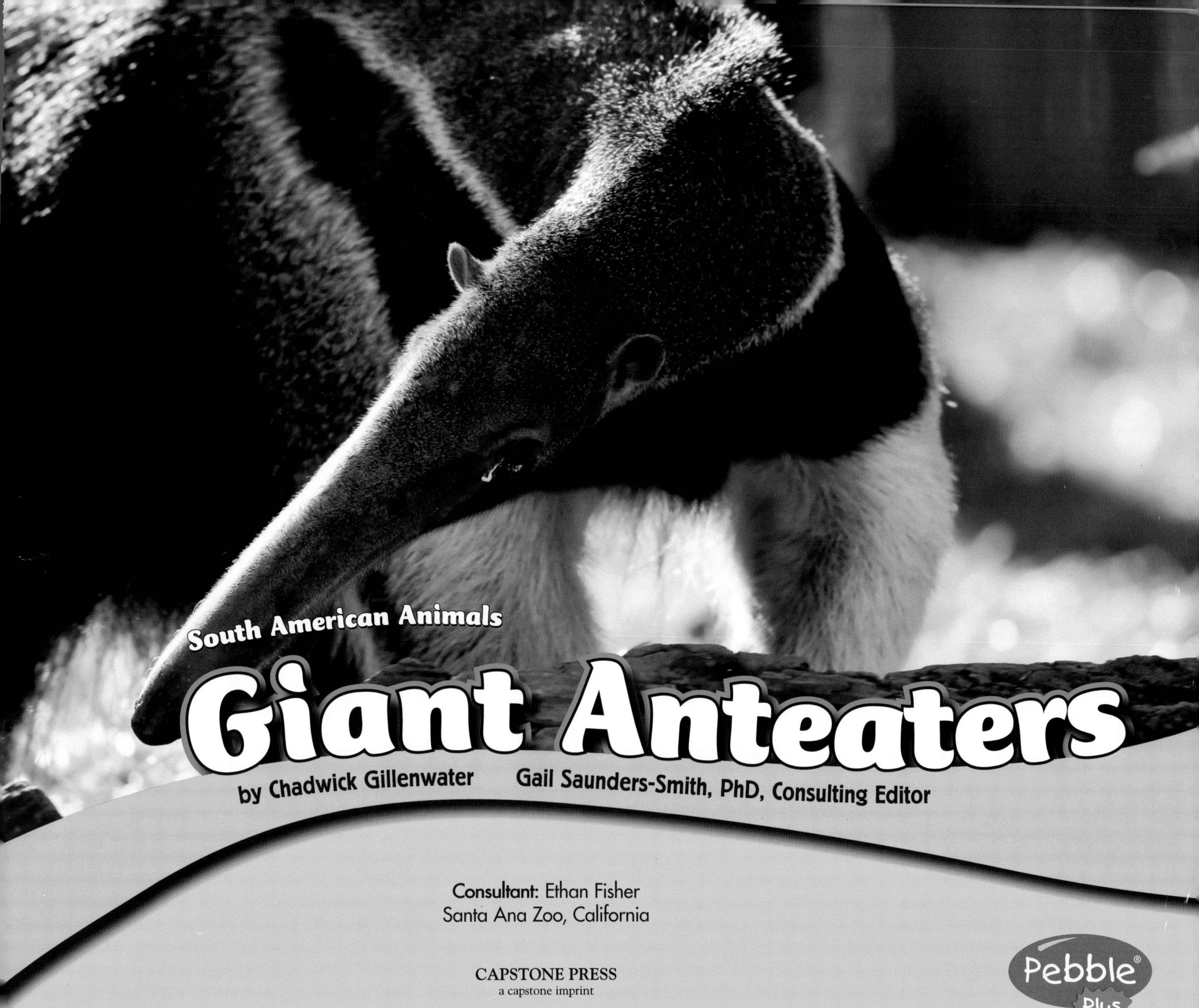

South American Animals

Giant Anteaters

by Chadwick Gillenwater   Gail Saunders-Smith, PhD, Consulting Editor

Consultant: Ethan Fisher
Santa Ana Zoo, California

CAPSTONE PRESS
a capstone imprint

Pebble® Plus

Pebble Plus is published by Capstone Press,
1710 Roe Crest Drive, North Mankato, Minnesota 56003.
www.capstonepub.com

Books published by Capstone Press are manufactured with paper containing at least 10 percent post-consumer waste.

Library of Congress Cataloging-in-Publication Data
Gillenwater, Chadwick.
Giant anteaters / by Chadwick Gillenwater.
p. cm.—(Pebble plus. South American animals)
Includes bibliographical references and index.
Summary: "Simple text and photographs present giant anteaters, how they look, where they live, and what they do"—Provided by publisher.
ISBN 978-1-4296-7587-1 (library binding)
1. Myrmecophaga—Juvenile literature. I. Title. II. Series.
QL737.E24G55 2012
599.3'14—dc23 2011027032

Editorial Credits
Katy Kudela, editor; Lori Bye, designer; Svetlana Zhurkin, media researcher; Kathy McColley, production specialist

Photo Credits
Alamy: All Canada Photos, 17, FLPA, 13, imagebroker, 5; Ardea: Keith and Liz Laidler, 21; Corbis: Theo Allofs, 9, Tom Brakefield, 15; Corel, 7; Dreamstime: Walter Arce, 1; Newscom: Danita Delimont Photography/Gavriel Jecan, 19; Photoshot: John H. Hoffman, 11; Shutterstock: lightpoet, cover

Note to Parents and Teachers

The South American Animals series supports national science standards related to life science. This book describes and illustrates giant anteaters. The images support early readers in understanding the text. The repetition of words and phrases helps early readers learn new words. This book also introduces early readers to subject-specific vocabulary words, which are defined in the Glossary section. Early readers may need assistance to read some words and to use the Table of Contents, Glossary, Read More, Internet Sites, and Index sections of the book.

Printed in the United States of America in North Mankato, Minnesota.
102011 006405CGS12

Table of Contents

Insect Catchers 4
Up Close! 8
Finding Food 12
Growing Up 16
Staying Safe 20

Glossary 22
Read More 23
Internet Sites 23
Index 24

Insect Catchers

Sniff. Slurp! A giant anteater gets a meal at an anthill. This South American mammal eats all day. It can slurp up to 30,000 insects a day!

World Map

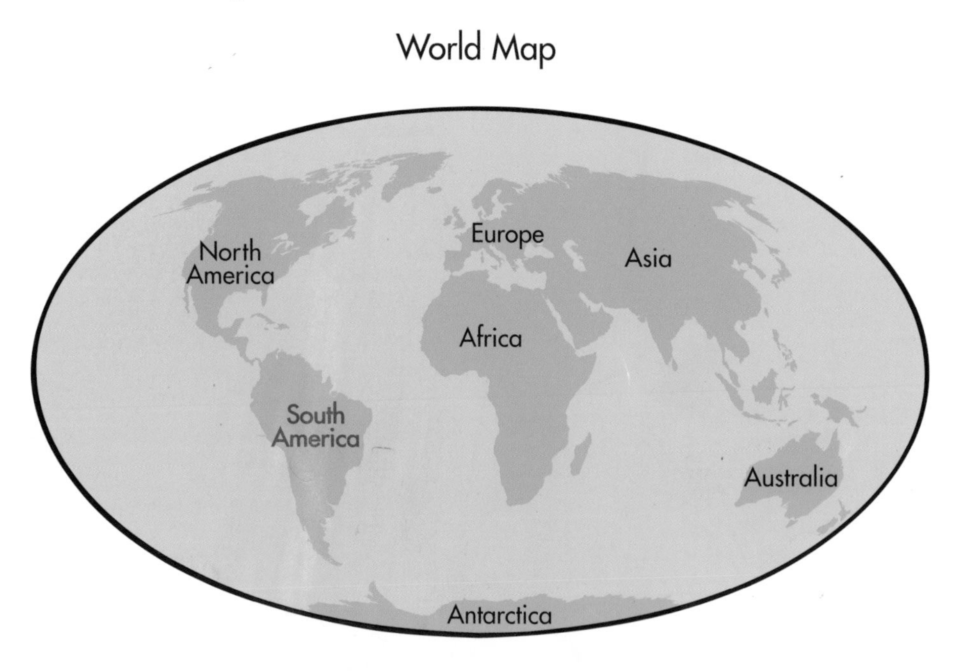

In South America, giant anteaters roam the rain forests. They hunt in grasslands too. These shy mammals live alone, except for mothers raising their young.

South America Map

where giant anteaters live

Up Close!

Giant anteaters have slim bodies with long snouts. From head to tail, they grow up to 7 feet (2.1 meters) long.

Giant anteaters have long, bushy tails. When sleeping, they drape their tails over their bodies like a fan.

Finding Food

Giant anteaters do not see well.
They use their noses to sniff
for anthills and termite mounds.
They use their claws to dig
holes in these nests.

Giant anteaters catch insects
on their long, sticky tongues.
Anteaters have no teeth,
but their stomachs grind
the food.

Growing Up

A female giant anteater gives birth to one baby at a time. A newborn pup weighs about 3 pounds (1.4 kilograms). For its first year, the pup rides on its mother's back.

Around age 2, a young anteater leaves its mother. It finds its own land to roam. Giant anteaters live about 15 years in the wild.

Staying Safe

Mountain lions and jaguars hunt anteaters. But anteaters fight back with their sharp front claws. Predators often leave to find easier prey.

Glossary

grind—to crush or wear down

insect—a small animal with a hard outer shell, six legs, three body sections, and two antennae; most insects have wings

jaguar—a large wildcat similar to a leopard, found in the southwestern United States, Mexico, and Central and South America

mammal—a warm-blooded animal that breathes air; mammals have hair or fur; female mammals feed milk to their young

predator—an animal that hunts other animals for food

prey—an animal hunted by another animal for food

snout—the long front part of an animal's head; it includes the nose, mouth, and jaws

termite—an antlike insect that eats wood

Read More

Allgor, Marie. *Endangered Animals of South America.* Save Earth's Animals! New York: PowerKids Press, 2011.

Antill, Sara. *Giant Anteater.* Unusual Animals. New York: Windmill Books, 2011.

Salas, Laura Purdie. *Mammals: Hairy, Milk-Making Animals.* Amazing Science. Animal Classification. Minneapolis: Picture Window Books, 2010.

Internet Sites

FactHound offers a safe, fun way to find Internet sites related to this book. All of the sites on FactHound have been researched by our staff.

Here's all you do:

Visit *www.facthound.com*

Type in this code: 9781429675871

Index

anthills, 4, 12
bodies, 8, 10
claws, 12, 20
eating, 4, 14
food, 4, 14
habitat, 6
hunting, 4, 6, 12, 14, 20
life span, 18
predators, 20
safety, 20
size, 8, 16
sleeping, 10
sniffing, 4, 12
snouts, 8, 12
South America, 4, 6
tails, 10
termite mounds, 12
tongues, 14
young, 6, 16, 18

Word Count: 216
Grade: 1
Early-Intervention Level: 19